MINDFUL MATES

"There will come a time when you believe everything is finished. That will be the beginning." ~ Louis L'Amour

Author Traci Baxendale Ball and editor Robert Ball own and operate Vibrant Health Company based in Marquette, Michigan. You can follow their Facebook page for insights into all things mental health @vibranthealthcompany. You can find them on Instagram @vibranthealthco

Website Address: https://vibranthealthcompany.com/

Traci also runs a successful health and fitness company called Vibe. See what Vibe is up to on Facebook @VibeLifeHealth and Instagram @vibelifehealth

Find the Author Bio in the back of this book.

●●● MINDFUL MATES

Weatherproof Your Romance.
Create Long-Term Love.

Traci Baxendale Ball

Text © 2019 by Traci Baxendale Ball

Edited by Robert Ball

Illustrations © 2019 by Traci Baxendale Ball

Design: Traci Baxendale Ball and Robert Ball

Graph on page 20 and 67 by Anonymous

Library of Congress Cataloging-in-Publication Data

Baxendale Ball, Traci
Mindful Mates - Weatherproof Your Romance. Create Long-Term Love
ISBN 978-0-692-06551-8 (paperback)
1. Couples Counseling-Therapy   2. Relationships-Communication   3. Sex-Sexual
Communication   4. Self Help   5. Marriage

Vibrant Health Company Press
118 W. Washington St. Ste. 2B
Marquette, MI 49855
(906)-273-2060
www.vibranthealthcompany.com

PB Printing   10 9 8 7 6 5 4 3 2 1

Contents

1   *Foreword*

5   *How to Use This Book*

7   *PART I- We Begin*

9   *Chapter 1: An Introduction to Couples Work*

21   *Chapter 2: Couples Work Assignments*

      23   *Assignment 1: Goal Setting*

      26   *Assignment 2: Fair Fighting*

      31   *Assignment 3: Actively Working On Forgiveness*

      41   *Assignment 4: Helping Your Partner With Their Goals*

45   *Chapter 3: Weatherproofing Your Romance*

59   *PART II- Let's Talk About Sex*

61   *Chapter 4: Intimate Monogamy: Overcoming Sexual Stagnation in Long-Term Relationships*

      63   *Re-Erect Your Sex Life*

65   *What to Expect in Normal Long-Term Relationships*

69   **Chapter 5: SexEd Assignments**

71   *Assignment 1: Owning Up to Sexual Difficulty or Neglect With Your Partner*

72   *Assignment 2: Our Intimacy Contract*

73   *Assignment 3: Intimacy Q and A*

78   *Boost Your Sex I.Q. - 17 Tips to Transform Sex From Mundane to Mind Blowing*

85   **Chapter 6: The Body Positive Movement**

87   *Body Love: Reclaiming Your Sexual and Sensual Self*

88   *Recommendations for Body Love*

97   **Author Bio**

FOREWORD

A note to my readers

Welcome! In a complicated world, what could be more important than learning to nourish and enrich your primary relationship? Thank you for taking the time to pick up this book in a world that is full of distractions!

Between 2015 and 2018, I field tested these materials with more than 700 clients in my private practice, which includes traditional in-person counseling as well as online coaching. I started writing this book in January of 2017 and continued to field test the materials, making adjustments based on feedback from clients. This year marks my 26th year as a social worker. I have collected a wealth of anecdotal information about human relationships. My clients have taught me well. I have also had my fair share of failures, both as a clinician and a significant other. I hope my stories and insights will give you the courage to work on your relationship.

It is common for couples to ask if I am married when they are trying to decide whether to sign up for my services. We all search for resonance. It seems important for people to know that I have experience as a single, a divorced, and now, a married-again person. I have been married three times. It took me that many attempts to get it right! It is within the context of my wonderful marriage that I offer you these materials. Long-term relationships are difficult to maintain and even more difficult to make great. I stuck with the title "Mindful Mates" because I want you to get back to the basics with your partner. Mindfulness offers you an opportunity to remember simple rules of thumb for relating to your life partner. These simple rules might spare you, my readers, the spiritual and financial upheaval of divorce.

Many of you work in the field as coaches, clinicians, practitioners, and healthcare professionals. However you label yourself, you all face the task of helping struggling couples. If you provide direct couples services and you're struggling to keep couples working toward resolution, my objective is to help YOU transform your practice with couples into a focused, effective, brief intervention with a designated beginning and end.

"Mindful Mates" was officially launched in 2017 as a brand of my company based in Marquette, Michigan. I've been using a collection of similar assignments, resources, and interventions as the ones you'll find in this book for years to 're-calibrate' couples. For most of my professional career, which began in 1992, I have lived and worked in small communities in the US. The availability of good couples counseling in these communities has always been marginal, but the reasons for that have changed. The barriers to having a greater number of talented clinicians providing couples counseling are numerous. Some are financial. For example, in the old days, it was very difficult to get reimbursed from insurance companies to perform couples counseling. Reimbursement was under the strict auspices of individual treatment with one person being the identified client and being assigned a diagnosis, even if the problem was that their partner was cheating on them. Many of these barriers have since been removed, although we are still required to give a diagnosis to one client in many cases.

Another barrier is training. Though we are all required to receive training on an annual basis for our license(s), there are very few offerings related to couples counseling at major state conferences unless one attends a specialized national conference such as AASECT. Getting specialized training is very expensive. Couples counseling can be an anxiety-provoking environment for even the most experienced helper. Contrary to individual work, there are multiple perspective takers at one time. The opportunity for therapeutic errors or transference is greater.

One reason for this book is that professionals offering couples counseling have very few validated, reliable handbooks or protocol-focused, skill-based, step-defined tools. This gap in our industry has left even the most committed professionals wading through couples sessions with no clear format or direction once the assessment is completed. This is frustrating for all, leaving us in a position where couples rehash the same topics over and over, literally paying a clinician for duplicates of conversations they have at home. David Burns, one of the most important clinical figures of our time, states that conversational-type traditional psychotherapy is not particularly effective. He prefers to arm clients with tools for rapid relief of issues. I wholeheartedly agree with his approach. Couples are often surprised when I tell them that it is not useful to show up for the session and argue for the entire hour, while I, the therapist, observes. After reviewing my guidelines, some couples decide that they simply want a space to fight. Though this may work well for some clinicians, I have found it to be detrimental for all involved.

Before I started this book, my husband and I were driving home after a typical workday. I told him that the art and science of couples counseling was so difficult that I felt there should be a rubric clinicians and coaches could follow. He replied, "You need an SOP, a standard operating procedure." Folks, this is it. Couples that sign up for my program know what to expect ahead of time, have an idea of the number of sessions it will take to reach resolution, and can look at the materials prior to services. I feel this gives potential clients an empowering start to what is often a difficult, emotional journey.

This book strives to provide professionals that want to enter, re-enter, or persevere in the minefield of couples counseling with an SOP that pulls together strategies from what the research says works. It aims to be a starter kit or foundation of sorts; one of the first systematic handbooks of how-to-do couples therapy that is GSD (Gender and Sexuality Diverse) competent. Clinicians that prefer a more fluid, intuitive approach will find a great deal of space for creativity within the suggested topics and assignments. Notice the word 'marriage' is omitted because it is necessary to be GSD aware and respectful of the myriad of ways that human beings can live as partners and families. The days of counseling only married, monogamous couples are over.

This book serves as a self-help tool for couples that are not able to or choose not to enter couples counseling. It can also be used effectively by individuals 'chipping away' alone at relational problems.

How to Use This Book

The book has two parts: Part 1 and Part 2.

<u>*Professionals*</u>

Professionals using the book can assign the tasks in sessions sequentially. Using them in this format gives you a sense of structure and direction in the couples counseling process. Some of the sections have universal value. Some of the sections (such as those on infidelity or sexual issues) may not apply to every client. In my practice, I generally use them in the order presented here. I give additional handouts with tips on mindfulness, cognitive therapy, date night ideas, and so on. Couples find great value in working on these tasks in session, sharing their answers, and capitalizing on the helper's skill. This information is used to facilitate solutions.

There are creative ways to use these assignments. They can be used quite easily in discussion groups, classes, and retreats.

<u>*Welcome, Self-Helpers*</u>

Couples and individuals have reported growth, insight, and resolution by working through the book without the help of a clinician.

Ideally, one section is completed each week. The idea is to read the explanation and complete the assignments alone or by working together. Time should be set aside for discussion with your primary partner where possible. If you are doing this alone and your partner is not participating, simply read each section and write in the blanks. It can be used as a journal for your relationship work. Some couples (or groups) choose to buy individual copies of the book, work in tandem on the assignments, then pause to share their insights. Once the assignment for the section you are working on is complete, be sure to discuss this with your partner before moving onto the next section.

Tip on Mindful Writing: The exchange of various written assignments between you and your partner is an idea that has been used for many decades in couples work. The basic idea is that you write to your partner and they write back. Many couples find that this gives them time to think carefully about what they want to say. It is a method of exchange that helps you both navigate sensitive topics. It alleviates the worry you may have about a heated discussion. Mindful writing demonstrates the turn taking employed by skilled communicators. When you learn the mindful writing technique using this workbook, you can take advantage of this powerful tool at any time in the future. Buy a large journal or notepad. Use it to write back and forth to each other. Alternatively, create a shared document on your devices to which you can both contribute. Mindful writing assignments improve the way you talk together because the turn taking represents the speaker and listener roles in a conversation.

PART I

WE BEGIN

"Nobody can go back and start a new beginning, but anyone can start today to make a new ending." ~ Maria Robinson

9

Chapter 1

An Introduction to Couples Work

"Connection is why we're here. We are hardwired to connect with others, it's what gives purpose and meaning to our lives, and without it there is suffering." ~ Brené Brown

Marriage Box

> Most people get married believing a myth that marriage is a beautiful box full of all the things they have longed for: companionship, intimacy, friendship, etc. The truth is that marriage at the start is an empty box. You must put something in before you can take anything out. There is no love in marriage. There is no romance in marriage. You have to infuse it into your marriage. A couple must learn the art and form the habit of giving, loving, serving, and praising, keeping the box full. If you take out more than you put in, the box will be empty.

You can't build a home that will withstand the elements without first building a foundation. You also need to be mindful about building a foundation before working on relationships. Consider this chapter your foundation.

Couples counseling is generally regarded in our field as the most difficult kind of talk therapy. Couples benefit from understanding this. The therapeutic balance is more difficult to establish and maintain than that between a clinician and solo client, or clinician and group. Expectations about what will happen in the course of counseling are often distorted. A classic example is as follows. At the end of the first session, when asked if they have any questions, a client will often ask the counselor, "So who's in the wrong? Whose fault is this? I thought you'd tell us that." Couples expect the counselor to take sides, even if they are not able to consciously recognize this fact. It's only human to want to be right. This makes holding a neutral space incredibly challenging for a clinician.

The stakes are high for couples entering counseling, which puts a great deal of pressure on the helper. For many couples, it's a last-ditch effort before permanently parting ways. Couples often enter counseling late in their journey of troubles. Research on the efficacy of couples counseling yields widely varying results. A 1987 study of 34 couples that received counseling resulted in 56% unchanged or deteriorated marriages, two years after counseling. ("Marital Therapy: 2-Year Follow-up and Prediction of Relapse," Journal of Marital and Family Therapy, Vol. 13, 1987.) But findings from a more recent study in the Journal of Marital and Family Therapy report that marriage counseling helped seven out of ten couples find great satisfaction in their marriage. (Research on the Treatment of Couple Distress," Journal of Marital and Family Therapy, Vol. 38, 2012.)

When I ask couples about their issues, there are common themes:

- Poor communication and destructive fighting.
- Differences in beliefs, values, attitudes, parenting, handling money, and relating to each other's family.
- Needing more time together; being generally overscheduled.
- Growing 'apart'; especially not having enough sex.

This book offers solutions in each of the problem areas.

Before Entering the Door of Couples Work: Do You Want to Stay Together?

I have established that couples counseling is one of the most difficult counseling modalities. Even couples that enter the door of counseling excitedly, and are matched with experienced professionals, will have a range of outcomes.

One of the problems with measuring the efficacy of couples counseling is that there is a bias or assumption that successful counseling will result in the couple staying in the relationship. This assumption is erroneous and often limits the perceived value of counseling. As clinicians, we need to operate from a different perspective: our job is to provide a fruitful space for insight. Based on this insight, individuals in the relationship can make informed decisions.

One of the first tasks to accomplish in couples counseling is to explore the motivation and intent of both individuals. It makes no sense to rush forward, intent on saving the relationship, if that is not what both people want. Some counselors meet with clients individually before couples counseling starts in an attempt to clarify the direction. This might be easier than trying to elicit the information during the first session with both parties present.

Who is Likely to Have 'Success' Using This Book?

Successful couples work should be seen as a process that brings individuals to an informed decision about their relationship, enabling a plan for the future. The plan may not include staying together. This book may help couples choose to stay together by exploring how to create a more mindful, peaceful, and meaningful relationship.

Certain conditions make it more likely you will be successful in staying together:

- You see the professional (and this book) as a 'neutral' consultant or resource rather than being the responsible party to fix your relationship.

- You are seeking help earlier rather than later in the story of your relationship troubles.
- You have **not** decided to end the relationship. You're still open to change and change work.
- Physical/emotional safety is, on the whole, assured in your relationship so that issues can be discussed without the threat of harm. Though you may have difficulty being transparent or vulnerable, your safety is not threatened if you do so.
- Your motivation to address problems in the relationship is high. From a motivational perspective on the 'readiness ruler', you would be sliding up toward the 'ready' end!

Not Ready ←---→ Ready

- Both partners feel that self-help or couples work can bring new information and help to a struggling relationship.

For Professionals

How to Set the Stage for Great Couples Work: Establishing Rules for Therapeutic Relationships

If you are working in the field as a helper for troubled couples, it is important to set the stage. I use the following creed to pre-load the possibility of in-session discomfort and conflict. This gives all parties a chance to cope ahead. Disagreement is seen as inevitable and is identified as part of the process rather than a reason to end the helping relationship early. If you decide to see a counselor, perhaps this will help you to see them as human and operating with good intentions. Reading this creed may help you to 'stick it out' with your counselor when you hit a rough patch.

Introduction - My Creed as a Clinician

Thank you for choosing me as your counselor. I want you to know that I always bring along my good intentions to our sessions. I also want you to know that I show up as myself. This means that at times I may say something you don't like or do something you don't like. I will make mistakes. This is more likely to happen in our early sessions, as you are getting used to my unique style and I am getting to know you. I want us to have a conversation now about how we will deal with it in the future when you disagree with me or feel troubled by what I say. This will help us all to relax in the session and bring authenticity to our work. We will discuss painful material together. You are putting yourselves 'out there', and I too must be willing to hear critical feedback. It will be difficult for us all, but worth it.

I decided to write this creed because over the years I have found that the greatest threat to doing good couples work is not being able to say what we mean and 'close the loop' when an issue comes up. The fact that our life experiences are different only enriches what we can learn from each other.

Creating a Contract With Your Counselor

Creating a contract between you, your partner, and your counselor is important. I have had more than a few challenges to these rules. However, when the rules are observed in the spirit of protecting your relationship, this correlates with the best outcomes for you.

Rules of Couples Counseling

- We understand that developing a relationship with you as a counselor will take a number of sessions. In those early sessions, we are all getting to know each other. This takes time. We will bear in mind your creed.
- During this process, we agree not to use the threat of divorce or leaving the relationship.
- We understand that the counselor <u>does not take sides</u> and is not here to tell my partner off. The goal is to help us navigate toward a resolution. The counselor will hold a neutral space.
- We will not punish each other for things said in counseling. If we need to talk about them outside the session, we will figure out a method that works. We agree that there is nothing off-limits in counseling, and we agree not to use dishonesty. This process only works if we can have transparency, truth, and honesty.
- We will now use the fair fight rules (found in Chapter Two of this book) to settle conflict and will embrace the chance to resolve issues rather than being afraid of disagreements.
- Are there any other rules you would like to establish right now?

What Are the Most Common Threats to a Happy Relationship?

- In first place by far, (for straight, monogamous couples), friendships with members of the opposite sex are a ticking time bomb. They may be work colleagues, exes, or friends on social media. This applies whether there was (or is) a physical connection, sexual talk, flirting, or platonic friendship. For non-traditional couples, (LGBTQIA+, poly or open relationships, non-monogamy) what causes trouble is poorly defined boundaries. This refers to poor communication in your relationship about how you will handle other friendships and a lack of compromise about them. Straight couples will often want to get into a philosophical discussion about how men and women can be friends. I agree this is possible. I don't agree that it is part of repairing a relationship. This is akin to saying you don't have to wear a seatbelt because you won't have an accident. As a counselor, I approach this from a more practical stance. If it causes your partner emotional pain, why would you do it? There are enough threats out there, make your relationship weatherproof!

- Unsatisfactory sex life.

- Poor communication.

- Destructive verbal and physical fights about family, money, and other high conflict topics.

Building Reasonable Expectations for Your Long-Term Love

Staying in love or falling back in love is an active, intentional process. Couples might think they must feel in love to stay with their partner. Couples think if they don't feel in love anymore their relationship is doomed. In many cases, the feeling can be created or recreated through action. When we recognize we would like to feel a certain way, we can generate this feeling through planning and action. This is called behavioral activation. Our success in being able to have great relationships over the long term does not depend on our feelings. We must hold on tight, do what works, and act skillfully as a partner.

What to Expect in Normal Long-Term Relationships

Relationships travel through predictable cycles. Understanding the ebb and flow of these cycles helps you to build reasonable expectations of your long-term romances. If you don't have reasonable expectations - if you don't understand what is normal - you may blame yourself or your partner when you hit inevitable lulls. A lull may be an extended period of time without sex. A lull may be a decrease in affection. A lull may be distancing or withdrawal. A lull may be being annoyed with your partner more often than in the past. You may think a lull marks the end of your love. Understanding that emotions wax and wane means you know sometimes you will feel disconnected from your partner, dislike them, and even hate them. Hope and patience create broad scope thinking. Broad scope thinking means you can think beyond what is happening right now. You should not make decisions based on whether you feel in love or not. Through an active process of mindfulness and relationship work, the next cycle of passion may be just around the corner. The sketch of the relationship cycle that follows was circulated at the 2017 AASECT conference in Las Vegas, NV (artist unknown). It tells the story of how relationships flow over time.

In the diagram, the first phase of the relationship is the infatuation phase, commonly referred to as the honeymoon stage. Studies vary when they explain how long this heady, exciting phase lasts. In general, it's a year or less. It might only be a few weeks. Usually, this phase is characterized by a strong sexual desire and almost obsessive thinking about your mate. All of their weaknesses are ignored, even when they are blindingly obvious. You feel like spending every waking moment together.

As infatuation subsides, you are more likely to see your true partner emerge. They fall from their proverbial pedestal, and you become a bit disillusioned. Nothing can replicate the lusty infatuation phase; that initial crazy time when you first fall in love. You can use the memories of this early NRE (new relationship energy) to fuel years of love with your partner and resist the temptation to look for it elsewhere because it is such a fleeting experience.

After the infatuation phase, which can be as long as a year but as short as a few weeks, partners are much more equipped to begin to assess for true compatibility. You start to evaluate the potential of the relationship outside of the all-encompassing experience of lust. There is a predictable phase where you realize your partner is human. You begin to see their flaws. Power struggles inevitably follow. As you surface for air, you have to learn about yourself as a partner to this person. You have to learn who they are as a partner to you. This is where couples earnestly learn how to communicate and how to resolve conflict. You begin to re-establish boundaries and a sense of self after the intense but unsustainable velocity of infatuation.

The last cycle shown in the diagram represents how healthy love undulates. Couples experience phases of being in love, but also experience lulls. To remain in your relationship and benefit from the security it offers, you must be able to tolerate periods of dissatisfaction. It is essential to embrace the highs and lows over the years to avoid common pitfalls. It is essential to savor good times with your long-term love and to sit tight through bad times without bouncing out of the circle altogether (ending the relationship).

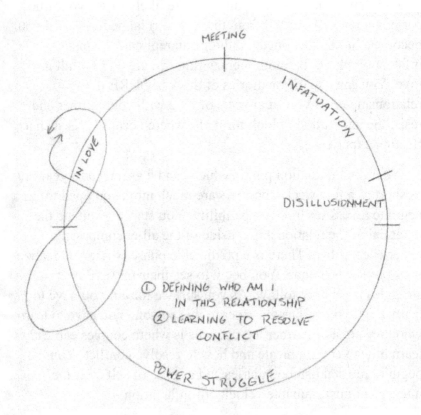

MEETING

INFATUATION

IN LOVE

DISILLUSIONMENT

① DEFINING WHO AM I
   IN THIS RELATIONSHIP
② LEARNING TO RESOLVE
   CONFLICT

POWER STRUGGLE

Chapter 2

Couples Work Assignments

"I define connection as the energy that exists between people when they feel seen, heard, and valued; when they can give and receive without judgment; and when they derive sustenance and strength from the relationship." ~ Brené Brown

Assignment 1: Goal Setting

My goals for our relationship are as follows:

1. Create reasonable expectations for Quality time together – amount & what does that look like?

2. Improve the way we communicate about dissatisfaction.

3. Come to a mutual understanding / expectation about money

4. Learn how to communicate about our sex life (Stosh says more sex)

5.

Miracle question for your relationship: Describe what it would be like if a miracle happened <u>right now</u> in your relationship and it is suddenly as good as it can get. Write in the space below. This will give you a target to move toward.

_____

_____

_____

_____

_____

_____

_____

_____

_____

What is standing in the way of you having an ideal, close connection?

1. _____

_____

2. _____

_____

3. _____

_____

4. _____

_____

5. _____

_____

Assignment 2: Fair Fighting

Read through the information on the following two pages about how to fight fair. Stick to your commitment. Don't let destructive fights or avoidance of conflict ruin your relationship. Print your rules. Post them as a reminder.

While we all know that violence is a relationship destructor, we don't always consider avoidance to be just as destructive. I believe it is. Apathy and avoidance may be quieter, but the effect on intimacy is the same.

The frequency of conflict in your relationship doesn't necessarily correlate with whether or not you will stay together. It's more about how you fight. Here are some suggestions for fighting fair.

Agree to stick to the rules before you fight.

Post them for easy visibility.

- One person talks at a time then pauses and breathes *instead of* more than one person talking or yelling or screaming.

- Sit down to resolve conflict as soon as it starts *instead of* standing up (which can lead to aggression), power trips, or destructive physical actions.

- Say what you want to happen, rather than blaming. "I want you to _____." *instead of* "Why didn't you_____?" Be straight and direct *instead of* expecting the other person to read your mind.

- Don't turn your back on the person talking. Look them in the eye and stop what you are doing *instead of* rejection with your body language.

- Focus on listening *instead of* your reply. Don't think about how to defend yourself.

- Use "I" sentences *instead of* "You, you, you."

- Focus on assertive, direct statements *instead of* abuse (name calling, put downs, cussing) or passivity (appearing uninterested), stonewalling (ignoring), and gas-lighting (saying things that question their sanity).

- Focus on the issue at hand *instead of* bringing up past instances and slights. Don't keep score.

- Leave family members and friends out of your argument *instead of* "You're just like your mother." "My friend says…" "My counselor says..."

- Stay present with your partner until there is resolution or agreement on when you can talk about it more *instead of* leaving, driving away, or threatening to leave. A relationship should never be under threat because of a problem that you both want to be resolved.

- Be willing to wave the white flag even if you are right *instead of* having the last word or proving your point. Remember you are on the same team.

- Never try to settle arguments using texting or hostile emails. It's easier to depersonalize and act badly. Don't air your relationship woes on social media. Keep your conflicts private.

   If your fights have become physical in any way, the priority is to restore safety in your relationship. You must be able to disagree and argue without violence and intimidation. Sit on your hands if you must. Stay out of your partner's personal space. Breathe through intense feelings. Take responsibility for your anger. Commit to the physical and emotional safety of your family.

Hurt, Forgiveness, and Repair

"Forgiveness does not change the past, but it does enlarge the future." ~ Paul Boese

What you do with this section can save your relationship. It is the most important part of this book. It's likely that this section will be the most difficult for you and your partner. Take your time.

Professionals: Your skill and savvy here can make or break your client's relationship. This part takes more sessions than any other section of this book when used in counseling. In my work with couples, this section often takes more than three sessions and as many as ten.

Couples feel awkward about stopping and starting their work in this section because of the emotional load. They wonder how to make space and time to do it and how to transition back into their ordinary lives after discussing such painful topics. After all, the apprehension about discussing old hurts is what gets couples into trouble in the first place. Creating structure around your work in this section may ease the tension. Structure may involve setting aside a day and time. Structure might include going to a peaceful location to complete the writing assignments. Structure may include an activity to smooth the transition from intense discussion to everyday life. My recommendation is that you pick a day and time to work on this section and use the same time each week until you're done. Show up on time for your partner. Pick a time when you're both less frazzled. I encourage you to have your talks in a neutral space, where you are physically close and can make eye contact. Privacy is paramount. Emotions will be strong. Once you have both had a turn as the speaker and you have both practiced the forgiveness script, ease back into your lives by going for a walk, getting coffee, or dining out.

30

The beauty of counseling is obvious here. It provides you with a neutral space, privacy, and a set date and time.

In this section, you will have a chance to tell your partner the hurts you've not been able to move past. They will be instructed on how to listen and respond. Similarly, your partner will have a chance to tell you how you have hurt them. You will need to use silence, active listening skills, reflection, and empathy. These skills will be used time and time again in your relationship. Though the skills don't come naturally to many, with practice and patience, you can learn to be a better communicator.

Resentments build up over the years like scar tissue. This prevents couples from being able to resolve issues both old and new. Before you focus on solutions and moving forward, you need to think about the topic of forgiveness. Forgiveness is an active process. It does not happen by accident. Assignment 3 shows you how to start.

Individuals in counseling often have a long list of resentments they need to resolve before moving forward. As a clinician, I've found that even the longest lists have themes. There may be many hurts caused by the same behavior.

If infidelity is part of your relationship story, there is a comprehensive assignment (Step 4 within Assignment 3) at the end of this chapter devoted specifically to this topic. It should be completed before this one.

Gabrielle Bernstein writes: "The miracle of forgiveness stems from an inner shift rather than an outer result. This means that forgiveness is less about the other person and more about you."

"The process of forgiveness is something you do for yourself. The other person doesn't even have to know that you forgive them." Gabrielle notes that "forgiveness sets the other person free to right their wrongs in the future" if you choose to let them know you forgive them.

Work through Assignment 3 which is based on Bernstein's model of forgiveness to set the stage for a 'clean slate' in your relationship. Your partner needs to be able to accurately reflect (which means re-state) your words and respond in an empathic manner. If they don't get it right, if they appear not to understand, it's okay to keep describing and explaining until they do have it right.

This section not only provides valuable work on resentment and forgiveness, but it also helps you practice good communication skills. You'll need to read through Steps 1 through 3 to understand how to use the questions and exercises effectively. Heed the warnings. Avoid common pitfalls.

Assignment 3: Actively Working on Forgiveness

Make a list of resentments or grudges you hold against your partner, no matter how far back in the past they happened. Think of the things they did that still hurt you. The list can be as detailed as you would like. Bear in mind writing is a powerful therapeutic task.

Keep your list in front of you. You will be talking about just one resentment on the list at a time. Save your list and use it the next time you sit down to work on this section with your partner. Remember that this section takes the most time and energy to finish.

Decide who will take their turn first at speaking. If you are listening, you are not permitted to talk while the speaker 'has the floor'. If you are listening, be aware of your body language. Do not dismiss your partner's hurt. It's likely that this lack of understanding has caused problems. Try to stay relaxed by breathing deeply. If possible, each person should take one turn being the speaker, then the listener. It's preferable to do only one resentment on your list at a time. Then stop. Don't try to get through your list in one round.

Use the questions in Step 1 to help you talk about <u>each resentment</u>. One partner takes the lead while the other listens. Remember to listen and learn, rather than defend. You need to face each other and maintain eye contact throughout the exercises.

Note: If you are completing this section alone, use this solitary time to pour your hurt and heart into your writing. Answer the questions in Step 1 and practice Step 2. Step 3 will not apply.

Step 1: Unearthing and working through emotional pain

- What relationships or memories still cause me to feel pain or sadness?
- What are the negative thoughts my mind turns to repeatedly?
- Who am I unwilling to forgive (including myself if applicable)?
- See your part. This may be difficult, especially if you were clearly wronged. In this case, your part may simply be holding on to anger. But if that's not the case, really take time to think about the role you played. How can you fix this?
- Change your mind. This is where you shift your thinking from negative to constructive and future-oriented, using the mantra in Step 2.

Tip: Conversations can be started like this: "It still hurts me when I think about_____." "I keep thinking about_____."

Step 2: Forgiveness mantra based on cognitive therapy

In this step, as the speaker, you use a script to help your mind shift from hurt to forgiveness. This does not mean you magically forgive your partner and your hurt is gone. It means you recognize you are actively working toward forgiveness, which is essential for a loving relationship.

Once you have spoken to your partner about your hurt and resentment, and they have responded based on the instructions in Step 3, you tell them:

"I forgive you and I release us from this pain."

This script marks the end of the discussion.

Tip: Use this script over and over as an affirmation whenever negative or painful thoughts arise or when you notice you are ruminating. An affirmation is an empowering statement you say to yourself.

Step 3: For the partner that's listening

The central question when you have caused hurt is: "How do I respond to the hurt I have caused, even if it was a long time ago and I thought they were over it?" The best response is always understanding. To understand, you must listen closely and try to put yourself in the speaker's shoes.

I've observed lots of listeners become impatient, even angry, with the speaker (their partner). They exclaim, "We've been through this!" "This was 30 years ago!" "You told me you let this go!" Listeners have stormed out of the session. Imagine what this does to the speaker, already anxious and displaying the courage to open up.

Your partner will feel less resentful if you show understanding and compassion. In this section of the work, there is no place for having the last word.

As you listen to your partner, the speaker, be silent. Try to understand their perspective, even if you don't think the details are correct. As the listener, try to re-state what you've heard once you're sure they have finished. Do not interrupt them or correct them.

Use this kind of language: "So are you saying _____?".

It is very important that once you can correctly re-state what you did to hurt them in the past, you then <u>stop talking</u>. You will need to pause to give your partner a chance to acknowledge whether you've got it right. It might take several attempts for you to get it right. Don't worry about that. Keep trying.

Here is where most mistakes are made and more damage is done. The listener, frantic to tell their side, starts constructing a response when the speaker starts talking. When the speaker, (their partner) stops, there is no consideration of what was said. Instead, the listener blurts out an explanation. Frequently the listener will say "Yes, but....".

I encourage you not to do that.

Once you are certain that you understand what the speaker is telling you, <u>because they tell you you've got it right</u>, you may answer any of the following questions. Some couples can proceed with this right away, but it's better to use the questions as a writing assignment that you show to your partner within a few days. Choosing to forgo your verbal reply, and instead writing out your response, has a more powerful effect. It implies you are not rationalizing your behavior, making excuses, or correcting them.

As the partner that caused the hurt, it is important that you reflect on and express the following:

- What conditions made you vulnerable to this behavior that caused them pain?

- What need did this behavior fill?

- Did you feel neglected in attention, affection, admiration, or appreciation? Why?

- You must be able to answer this question: "How much have I hurt you?"

Understand it is the adequacy of your empathy that will help your partner heal.

As you progress through painful material, work hard to communicate using the Fair Fighting Rules.

Step 4: Establishing a foundation of trust after infidelity

Working through Steps 1–3 within Assignment 3 is essential for all couples. Step 4 is only for couples that are working through the painful reality of infidelity.

Couples attempting to stay together after an affair face a huge hurdle when it comes to forgiveness. Some individuals need very little information to begin to move past their hurt. More often, individuals have many questions that they feel are critical to their healing process.

Couples often want clarification on what 'counts' as infidelity. Infidelity or cheating always involves deceit, secrecy, emotional connection, and often involves sexual behavior.

My clients report struggling with painful memories for a year or more after they discover their partners' infidelity.

Once infidelity is discovered, you may notice whoever was cheated on is suspicious about where you are, what you are doing, and who you are with. The best approach is transparency. As the partner that was hurt by infidelity, be clear about what you need to know to feel secure. As the partner that caused the hurt, be forthcoming. Tell them where you are, who you are with, and when you will be home. Hand over your phone. Try to avoid lengthy separations in the early days of relationship restoration. Stick to the rules I explained at the beginning of the book.

If infidelity is part of your relationship story, highlight any of the following questions you feel would be useful to ask your partner. Give them time to answer thoroughly without butting in. Once your partner has had a chance to answer, your job is to reflect back what they have said to ensure you heard correctly. Remember this clarifying question: "So are you saying_____?"

This material is painful to say and hear. It will take all your energy to get through this assignment. Show kindness to yourself and plan to rest afterward.

Finding the meaning behind an affair can help you with a framework for recovery. These questions help open up dialog. 'Meaning' is not about shifting blame, it doesn't mean you excuse your partner's actions. This is an insight-oriented assignment to gain perspective. Take as much time as needed to cover the questions that are important to you.

This step attempts to capture the many questions couples posed to each other during my sessions over the years. Most couples benefit from the balancing, soothing presence of a professional as they navigate this difficult step. I *have* seen some couples get through this assignment alone. If I don't have both parties in counseling, my strategy is to give the interested individual or couple a list of the questions to take home. I prep them and let them know the level of difficulty of the assignment and that it can take several hours to complete.

A list of questions my clients asked their partners who cheated on them:

- What made that time in our relationship vulnerable to infidelity?
- What did you tell yourself to convince yourself that it was okay to act like that?
- Was this an 'emotional affair' or did you have some kind of physical sexual contact? Do you think it could have gone even further than it did? Why or why not?
- Who initiated it?
- Who ended it and how did it end?
- What will you do if this person tries to contact you?
- Did the connection provide something that you felt you needed? Why couldn't you ask me to provide that?
- What else did you get out of it that you weren't getting in our relationship?
- Were you getting some need met from this other person that I cannot possibly provide?
- Did you feel guilty? Do you feel guilty now?
- You knew it was wrong, how could you let it go on for so long?
- What did you learn from it?
- Is there anyone else that you believe shares the blame for this?
- What made it difficult to stop?
- What did you tell them about us?
- Did the affair have anything to do with something you felt was missing from our sex life?

- Did you ever want me to find out? Were you hoping I would, and this would stop it?
- Why did you tell me about the affair? -OR- Why didn't you tell me about the affair?
- What drew you to this person?
- Were you ever worried about losing me?
- What do you want me to know about the affair?
- How did you feel when I found out about the affair?
- Did you want me to find out about your affair?
- Did you think I would never find out?
- What was it like to keep the affair a secret?
- How did you make time for them when we were already busy?
- What was it like to come home to me?
- Did you see a future with this other person?
- Did you ever think of leaving me?
- Did you ever want to leave me?
- Are you staying for me or are you staying for the children or some other aspect of life together?
- Do you think it will happen again?
- Do you understand how I feel?
- Are you willing to give me time to recover?
- What would it be like for you if I had an affair?
- How long do you think it will take for me to get over this? What will make that happen in your opinion?
- Do you think you can live by the relationship rules to protect us from outside insults to our relationship?

Questions clients asked each other:
- Do you think you can ever trust me again?
- Do you still want me in your life? In what role?

- Do you think we can repair our relationship?
- Do you think you can move past this?
- What commitments do we need to make now?
- What needs to change?
- If we were to walk away from our relationship, what would you miss the most?
- How can I help you heal?

Questions clients asked when they cheated:
- Why do you choose to work on this relationship rather than leaving?
- How can I help you feel more hopeful about us?
- What can I do to help you start to trust me again?
- Do you believe me when I say I am sorry?
- What do you want me to do when you are having doubts or having a hard time?

Please list any other questions you have below:

1. _____

2. _____

3. _____

4. _____

5. _____

Assignment 4: Helping Your Partner With Their Goals

Read your partner's goals from Assignment 1 and formulate your responses:

"I can be part of the solution in our relationship by doing these things:"

Make a list of the things you are willing to do to help your partner with their goals.

1. _____

_____

2. _____

_____

3. _____

_____

4. _____

_____

5. _____

_____

6. _____

_____

7. _____

_____

8. _____

_____

9. _____

_____

10. _____

_____

We will now move on to constructing a more mindful framework for your relationship that is solid and able to withstand 'bad weather'.

Let's work on solutions. Let's get mindful!

Congratulations! You have worked through the most challenging and emotionally draining material. If you are still engaged in the process and have hope that your relationship can survive, the odds are very good at this point.

You identified relationship goals and obstacles to those goals. Look back on them and see if they are still relevant. How do you think you are doing?

Chapter 3

Weatherproofing Your Romance

"Mindfulness is simply being aware of what is happening right now without wishing it were different; enjoying the pleasant without holding on when it changes (which it will); being with the unpleasant without fearing it will always be this way (which it won't)." ~ James Baraz

Weatherproof Your Relationship With Mindfulness

Being a good partner is a lot of work. There is no magic. There is no one-time fix.

Weatherproofing, when it comes to relationships, means doing what you can to make your relationship more resilient. It also means minimizing possible exposure to toxins. 'Weatherproof Your Relationship' is my catchphrase, and I encourage you to visualize 'spraying down' your relationship with these mindfulness skills.

Mindfulness means being in the moment. Being mindful in a relationship is about being thoughtful, connected to, and mirroring your partner. Mindfulness leads to better communication.

Getting professional help is cheaper than divorce. If you're finding it difficult to learn the essentials of communication through self-help, seek out a good counselor that can help you be a super communicator.

Patterns of behavior with your partner may have started long ago. They could represent inherited dynamics from your family of origin. Behaviors can be divided into pro-relationship actions and relationship-destroying actions. The idea is to eliminate relationship-destroying actions (violence, withdrawal, infidelity, passivity) and to increase pro-relationship actions (affection, dating, good communication, great sex).

The following basic mindfulness skills are a good start for anyone who wants to create more pro-relationship routines:

1. Active Listening

"Communication is the fuel that keeps the fire of your relationship burning. Without it, your relationship goes cold."
~ William Paisley

Unfortunately, until you learn active listening skills, you do not listen to understand. You listen to react and defend. To be a good communicator you have to drop your normal listening style which is reactive. As one client said after learning about active listening:

"All this time I thought I was communicating with my wife, but I think I've just been talking. I've not been hearing her at all."

Active listening helps you to shut off the chatter and drop the defense you naturally mount in your mind. It helps you to be in the moment with your partner. You can show your partner you have 'heard' them by repeating back what they say. You re-state their words. This is called a reflection. You can practice this in session with your counselor. When you practice active listening, reflections, and assertive communication with your partner, it will feel foreign at first. In the early stages of practice, to give yourself time to pause and think, you will use the same sentence stems again and again: "So what you're saying is_____." or "So are you saying_____?". As time passes and you become better at listening, you will be able to move away from these formal phrases that might seem canned or cheesy. You will develop your own language and style. Your partner will develop them as well. Eventually, this new way of talking and listening to each other will be a habit. You will seek clarity when listening. Use humor and humility as you stumble around in the early stages of your practice. Take extra time.

If you find yourself responding too quickly, especially if you are prone to anger, you need to make space between your thoughts and your response. I will discuss this in more detail shortly.

Tip: Remember the definition of reflective listening: a communication strategy involving two key steps. First, seek to understand the speaker's idea, then offer the idea back to the speaker to confirm the idea has been understood correctly.

2. Relinquish the Desire to Fix It

Hole in the Wall Metaphor (see box)

If you find that you respond quickly with a solution when your partner tells you about a problem, use my 'hole in the wall' metaphor to understand that what they want you to do is *just listen*. You don't have to fix it. You do need to hear. Using this metaphor will help if you try to fix the problem instead of listening. Remember you are listening only to understand.

Hole in the Wall Metaphor

When your partner brings something up for discussion, imagine (visualize) you stand by them, and together you gaze at a wall. Your partner says there is a hole in the wall. They point to it. You are already thinking about grabbing your toolbox and patching it up. Instead, you stand, gently fold your arms, assume a contemplative stance, and gaze at the wall with them. This demonstrates the art of listening, the basis for intimacy, empathy, and great relationships. © Vibrant Health Company

---

3. Dosing with reality

Mindfulness (being aware of your behavior) can help you avoid the common pitfall of dosing your partner with reality. This is the "I told you so" attitude. If you tend to dose your partner with reality when they report a failure, use the hole in the wall metaphor. Discard the smug attitude. Be on your partner's side. Listen skillfully.

As one client said to their partner in session:

> *"Please make this about me just this once, not your reality check!"*

4. Practice the Stop, Pause, Breathe Technique.

In this book, a common theme is pausing when you communicate. Pausing to add a breath as you're talking with your partner is the most important behavior you can learn to make your communication better. When you can pause, you can think. When you can think, your communication is measured rather than impulsive. Breathing helps you feel less tense. Once you pause, you may realize what you're about to say is a bad idea.

5. Sometimes the Best Thing to Say is Nothing at All.

Having the last word is not necessary. It's important to hold your tongue if you're about to use cruelty, sarcasm, or make a snide remark. Silence should not be used as a punishment. Weigh your next best move with a pause and a breath. There is a Sufi saying that goes like this:

"Before you speak, let your words pass through three gates: Is it true, is it necessary, is it kind?"

6. Apologize.

Say you are sorry when it is necessary. Never add 'but'. If you add 'but', your apology is null and void. If you feel clarification on your behavior is needed, you can talk about it later.

If what you did was serious, don't ask for forgiveness. Instead, ask what you can do to earn back trust. It's okay to say, "I hope you can forgive me." Do not demand forgiveness. Remember your partner may need time. Accept responsibility for what you did and the hurt you caused.

7. Vulnerability

Vulnerability increases connection and intimacy. Vulnerability is closely related to the idea of authenticity and being real with your partner, as well as yourself.

If you have difficulty opening up, you might tell others "I don't like to talk about feelings", or "I'm a private person". While zipping up in this way has many uses, it does not serve you in long-term relationships. It could be blocking your ability to communicate and let your partner in.

Answer these questions:

- Trusting someone makes me feel vulnerable because:

  _____

  _____

- Experiencing this kind of vulnerability would:

  _____

  _____

- Staying closed off serves the purpose of:

  _____

  _____

- This is how I stay closed off:

  _____

  _____

- Our relationship has been affected in the following ways by my refusal to be vulnerable:

_____

_____

- I contemplate changing that now after all this time because:

_____

_____

- One thing I'd like to open up more about is:

_____

_____

- My partner can show respect to me and value me by:

_____

_____

If you're not a 'talker' and your partner wants you to talk more, you might feel at a loss about how to start. You might feel you have nothing to say. When clients bring this problem up in session, I ask them to do three things. First, be curious about your partner. Practice this curiosity by asking them questions. In general, people like answering questions about themselves; at least in the context of a loving relationship. Imagine you are a journalist writing an article on the topic of your partner. What would you need to know to write with authority? Secondly, scour the internet for handy lists of conversation starters. Write down questions you like. Thirdly, ask your partner if there is anything they would like to know about you. What do they wonder about from time to time?

Bear in mind that without conversation, intimacy is limited.

8. Eye Contact

Eye contact increases connection, intimacy, and sexual fire. When is the last time you really looked into your partner's eyes? The answer may surprise you. Your counselor can give you simple tasks to increase your comfort level with eye contact. You might practice in session. You can also practice by yourself at home. Be mindful about looking at your partner when they are talking to you. Try the four-minute eye contact experiment: sit facing your partner. Breathe as you hold your partner's eye contact for four minutes. The rule is you must stay silent. Talk about how you felt during the four-minute experiment with your partner.

Notice how the four-minute eye contact experiment makes your partner more likable and attractive.

9. Simple Daily Mindful Tasks & Pro-Relationship Activities

In addition to learning how to listen well, how to resolve conflict, and how to open up, consider using this list as a guide to further weatherproof your relationship and maintain long-term love.

- A compliment to your partner each day keeps disconnection at bay. Say something nice.
- Make time for a connected and relaxed (not distracted or mindless) conversation every single day.
- Date your partner. Take responsibility to plan lunch, dinner, or dessert for just the two of you. Get creative and ditch dining out. Play in the great outdoors together or learn a new hobby. Explore a nearby town.
- Be mindful that this relationship is your job. Love is an active process, not a dumping ground for your worst moments, bad breath, and apathy. Don't assume your partner wants the leftovers of you after everyone else has had their piece.
- Your partner is your teammate, not your enemy. Think: "We're on the same side.", no matter what.
- Delay conversations that may be fraught with tension until at least an hour after you get home. Ease into your time together. Don't walk in the door with immediate complaints. Bring up gripes after you've had a chance to share some positive news.
- No mind reading allowed. Learn how to be direct with your requests, likes, and dislikes. Ask for what you want. Say "I want _____." or "Can we _____?" and "I'd like to_____." Put away romantic notions that your partner should somehow know what you want. Be clear. Use fewer words for more impact.
- Don't be passive about the most important relationship in your life. Think of your relationship as a conscious breathing animal that needs nurturing and continuous care.

- Keep having sex. If you don't feel like it, read on. The rest of this book is for you.
- If you're not sure how to be more active and mindful in your relationship, do what you would normally do when you want to learn: study. Approach this like a research project. The best books out there to help are:

Mindful Mates- Baxendale Ball, T.E. (2018) Marquette, MI: Vibrant Health Company Press.

12 Hours to a Great Marriage- Markman, H.J., Stanley S.M., Blumberg, S.L., Jenkins, N.H., & Whitely, C., (2003) San Francisco, CA: Jossey-Bass.

Assisted Loving- Morris, B. (2008) New York, NY: Harper Collins.

Hot Monogamy- Love, P. & Robinson, J. (1995) New York, NY: Penguin.

Men are from Mars Women are from Venus- Gray, J. (1992) New York, NY: Harper Collins.

Designer Relationships- Michaels, M.A. & Johnson, P. (2015) Jersey City, NJ: Cleis Press. (Author's note- This is poly/LGBTQIA competent.)

The Power of a Praying Wife- Omartian, S. (1997) Eugene, OR: Harvest House.

The Five Love Languages- Chapman, G. (1995) Chicago, IL: Northfield.

Fighting for your Marriage- Markman, H.J., Stanley, S.M., Blumberg, S.L. (1994) Hoboken, NJ: Wiley Press.

Divorce Busting- Weiner-Davis, M. (1992) New York, NY: Simon and Schuster.

CPR for your Sex Life- Brown, M.L. & Braveman, S.L. (2007) Charleston, SC: Booksurge.

7 Principles for Making Marriage Work- Gottman, J.M. & Silver, N. (1973) New York, NY: Three Rivers Press.

Mirror of Intimacy- Kalehakis, A. & Bliss, T. (2014) CreateSpace Independent Publishing Platform.

She Comes First- Kerner, I. (2009) New York: Harper Collins.

10. Ideas for the Future

What are your ideas for transforming your relationship into a more mindful and fulfilling one? Exchange your ideas with your partner.

- _____

- _____

- _____

- _____

- _____

Part II

LET'S TALK ABOUT SEX

"I love you not only for what you are, but for what I am when I am with you." ~ Ray Croft

Chapter 4

Intimate Monogamy: Overcoming Sexual Stagnation in Long-Term Relationships

"If there is no passion in your life, then have you really lived? Find your passion, whatever it may be. Become it, and let it become you and you will find great things happen FOR you, TO you, and BECAUSE of you." ~ Kute Blackson

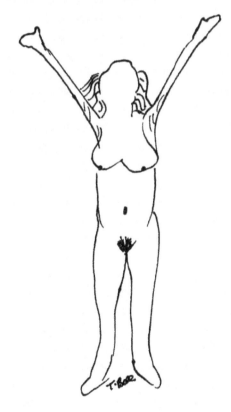

Re-erect Your Sex Life

Almost every couple I meet with reports trouble with their sex life. Having a robust sex life diminishes trouble spots in every other area of focus such as communication and conflict resolution. Sex is indeed the best lubricant for a relationship. Sex is not the same as intimacy. Intimacy is made up of many things. Most of all, it means you can be vulnerable with your partner. Intimacy is achieved when you share your mind and heart. It is difficult to achieve true intimacy without the glorious sharing of your body which happens in sex.

This part of the book focuses on enhancing or fixing your sex life. Many couples choose to complete Part II without their counselor because of discomfort talking openly about the sexual issues they have faced. Sadly, opportunities are missed for candid work on one of the most important dimensions of successful long-term love.

I encourage you to discuss any sexual concerns directly with the person you've employed to help you. For many of us working in the field, finding solutions to sexual problems is a routine part of our day, and we are quite comfortable discussing your concerns. There are real, evidence-based solutions, practices, and products for common sexual problems such as premature ejaculation, skin irritation in the vulva area, painful sex, fear of sex, and pelvic floor issues. Please don't be afraid to ask for help.

I'm often asked how to refresh sexual fire in long-term, monogamous relationships. As New Relationship Excitement (NRE) decreases, relationships settle into the comfort of coupled life. The sexual and sensual enjoyment between partners naturally decreases and takes more work to enjoy. Couples remember the first stage of the relationship when they had sex daily or more. By the time the couple lands in my office, they may not be having any sexual contact at all.

If you read the first section of this book, you will know that your expectations of long-term love are an important foundation. Your expectations help you decide whether to minimize the symbolic meaning of a rough patch or make it grounds for separation. It's worth reviewing again. Staying in love or falling back in love is an active, intentional process. Couples might think they must feel in love to stay with their partner. Couples think if they don't feel in love anymore, their relationship is doomed. In many cases, the feeling can be created or recreated through action. When we recognize we would like to feel a certain way, we can generate this feeling through planning and action. This is called behavioral activation. So much of our success in being able to have great sex over the long term depends not on feelings, but on putting together a plan for maintaining sex and following through. I will show you how.

Repair of sexual relations is more complicated when there are trauma-related sexual issues such as a history of sexual assault, infidelity, or sex addiction. Such cases may require individual counseling for the survivor and the partner, as well as couples work. These issues are beyond the scope of this book.

Achieving a satisfying sex life starts with the realization of its central importance to your emotional well-being and overall relationship satisfaction. With this realization, you can verbalize your intent to your partner. You can focus on your commitment to move toward a more vital sense of self. If you and your partner are suffering from an extended period without sexual contact, Assignment 1 in Chapter 5 is a conversation starter that can be used to have a conversation or express yourself in writing.

Tip: The exchange of various written assignments between you and your partner is an idea that has been used for many decades in couples work. The basic idea is that you write to your partner and they write back. Many couples find that this gives them time to think carefully about what they want to say.

What to Expect in Normal Long-Term Relationships

Relationships travel through predictable cycles. Understanding the ebb and flow of these cycles helps you to build reasonable expectations of your long-term romances. If you don't have reasonable expectations - if you don't understand what is normal - you may blame yourself or your partner when you hit inevitable lulls. A lull may be an extended period of time without sex. A lull may be a decrease in affection. A lull may be distancing or withdrawal. A lull may be being annoyed with your partner more often than in the past. You may think a lull marks the end of your love. Understanding that emotions wax and wane means you know sometimes you will feel disconnected from your partner, dislike them, and even hate them. Hope and patience create broad scope thinking. Broad scope thinking means you can think beyond what is happening right now. You should not make decisions based on whether you feel in love or not. Through an active process of mindfulness and relationship work, the next cycle of passion may be just around the corner. The sketch of the relationship cycle that follows was circulated at the 2017 AASECT conference in Las Vegas, NV (artist unknown). It tells the story of how relationships flow over time.

In the diagram, the first phase of the relationship is the

infatuation phase commonly referred to as the honeymoon stage. Studies vary when they explain how long this heady, exciting phase lasts. In general, it's a year or less. It might only be a few weeks. Usually, this phase is characterized by a strong sexual desire and almost obsessive thinking about your mate. All of their weaknesses are ignored, even when they are blindingly obvious. You feel like spending every waking moment together.

As infatuation subsides, you are more likely to see your true partner emerge. They fall off of their proverbial pedestal, and you become a bit disillusioned. Nothing can replicate the lusty infatuation phase; that initial crazy time when you first fall in love. You can use the memories of this early NRE (New Relationship Energy) to fuel years of love with your partner and resist the temptation to look for it elsewhere because it is such a fleeting experience.

After the infatuation phase, which can be as long as a year but as short as a few weeks, partners are much more equipped to begin to assess for true compatibility. You start to evaluate the potential of the relationship outside of the all-encompassing experience of lust. There is a predictable phase where you realize your partner is human. You begin to see their flaws. Power struggles inevitably follow. As you surface for air, you have to learn about yourself as a partner to this person. You have to learn who they are as a partner to you. This is where couples earnestly learn how to communicate and how to resolve conflict. You begin to re-establish boundaries and a sense of self after the intense but unsustainable velocity of infatuation.

The last cycle shown in the diagram represents how healthy love undulates. Couples experience phases of being in love, but also experience lulls. To remain in your relationship and benefit from the security it offers, you must be able to tolerate periods of dissatisfaction. It is essential to embrace the highs and lows over the years to avoid common pitfalls. It is essential to savor good times with your long-term love and to sit tight through bad times without bouncing out of the circle altogether, (ending the relationship).

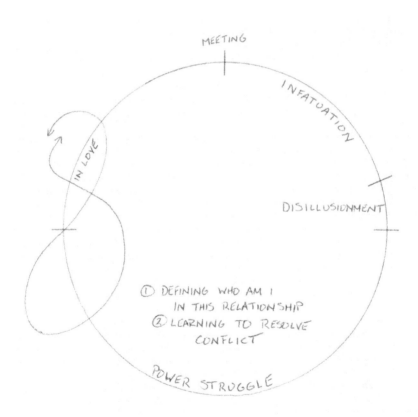

Chapter 5

SexEd Assignments

"As I learn to love myself, I automatically receive the love and appreciation that I desire from others. If I am committed to myself and to living my truth, I will attract others with equal commitment. My willingness to be intimate with my own deep feelings creates the space for intimacy with another." ~ Shakti Gawain

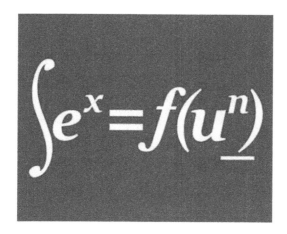

It's Time for a Candid Talk About Sex

Assignment 1: Owning Up to Sexual Difficulty or Neglect With Your Partner

You now have an understanding of the central importance of sex in your relationship. If sex has been on the back burner and especially if your partner is expressing resentment due to not having frequent sex, use these statements to start a conversation about turning over a new leaf. Think of this as an apology. Set intentions for the future.

Write the following on a piece of paper. Putting this in a heartfelt card is also a nice gesture.

I am sorry I have neglected your sexual needs.

It's been difficult for me to have sex with you because:

1. _____

   _____

2. _____

   _____

3. _____

   _____

4. _____

_____

5. _____

_____

I love you and I am working on this.

I am committed to having a satisfying sex life.

Next, read the Intimacy Contract in Assignment 2 to help you start a dialog about sex. Discuss the bullet points if you'd like. Assignment 2 helps you figure out what you can do to communicate about sex more confidently.

Assignment 2: Our Intimacy Contract

(Adapted from the groundbreaking bestselling book **Hot Monogamy**. Love, P & Robinson, J. (1995) New York, NY: Penguin.)

I recognize that to improve our sex life, we have to be able to communicate openly about sex. This means I will need to learn to:

- State my needs and expectations clearly
- Talk about sex more often

- Listen to what you have to say
- Ask about your wants, your needs, and your desires
- Be receptive to 'in the moment suggestions' about my technique
- Ask about my technique and adapt it to what feels good
- Reframe irrational thoughts about sex/my body
- Avoid criticism and sarcasm about sex; recognize this is different from communication and humor
- Accept roadblocks as being normal

Then, move onto Assignment 3. Write in your answers. Talk about them with your partner.

Assignment 3: Intimacy Q and A

1. The first thing I found sexually attractive about you was:

_____

_____

2. One of our best ever sexual experiences was:

_____

_____

3. My favorite time to make love is:

_____

_____

4. A sexual activity I'd like to try is:

_____

_____

5. In terms of sex, I wish I were better at:

_____

_____

6. What I would like more of in our love-making is:

_____

_____

7. What I'd like less of in our love-making is:

_____

_____

8. Something I find difficult to discuss is:

_____

_____

9. Something that concerns me about our sexual relationship

   is:_____

   _____

10. What I would like to know about you and sex is:

    _____

    _____

11. What still turns me on about you is:

    _____

    _____

12. I am committed to making the best of our love-making

    because: _____

    _____

Libido Lifter: Tips to Address Your Sagging Desire

Sex should be fun, so I've added humor liberally to the remainder of my book.

We move on to specifically address low libido and lack of desire for sex. The medical term for this is Hypoactive Sexual Desire Disorder. In this section, we will talk about managing HSDD.

A common question is "What can I do to feel like having sex more often?"

Libido means life force. When you feel life force, you'll naturally want more sex. You are a busy person. Your life is stressful. All that background noise drowns out time for self-reflection and self-awareness.

Increased libido is not only about wanting more sex. When you lose the connection with your inner self, you forget what makes you thrive. When you don't do things that make you thrive anymore, it's harder to connect to your sensuality. When you don't feel sensual, you don't feel sexual.

To increase your libido, you must gradually reawaken the self. You must develop an understanding of how a healthy self-esteem and body image contributes to wanting sex more often. You must recognize that broad issues in wellness such as insomnia, medications, depression, stress, and lack of physical activity dampen your desire for sex. If these areas of wellness are trouble spots for you, consider seeking professional care which can help you establish balance. Research suggests mind-body approaches such as yoga, mindfulness, and meditation can wake up the sex drive.

Do I Need to See a Doctor About My Sex Problems?

Sex problems with your partner go beyond procrasturbation (putting off what you can do today and stalling by engaging in masturbation).

You should always let your doctor know your concerns. Typical sexual issues that clients identify include premature ejaculation, lack of sex drive, erectile dysfunction, and pain during penetration. Some tests can be performed to check for structural issues such as lesions, fibroids, or endometriosis. You may be suffering from hormone imbalance. There are new medications to treat low libido in women. Viagra® and Flibanserin® are the most commonly prescribed. There are a few medications to treat erectile dysfunction in men. At the time of press, these medications are sildenafil (Viagra®), vardenafil (Levitra® or Staxyn®), tadalafil (Cialis®), and avanafil (Stendra®). Penile injections have been used with some success. Alprostadil (Caverject® or Edex®) is injected directly into the side of the penis and produces an erection. Natural remedies and pumps are alternatives for men who cannot use these medications.

Once your medical provider has assessed you and ruled out a medical cause, a counselor can help with products and interventions to resolve your sexual issues.

Mindfulness, Affection, and Sex

90% of couples that enter counseling report they want a better sex life. It's a primal need that gets suppressed if you're over-extended. Your existence on earth relies upon the biology of attraction and sex. You may have become disconnected from this important aspect of long-term relationships. Sex is bonding. So is affection. Be mindful about affection and sex in your relationship. If you are not naturally affectionate, you can learn to be, just as you have learned to be a good communicator using the assignments in this book. If you're not naturally good at sex, you can learn to be. Use the tips in the next section.

Are you new to mindfulness? It's about living in the moment. It's about slowing down so you can be aware of your own needs and those of your partner. It's about focusing on here and now. Don't let opportunities to show affection pass you by. This is especially important if your partner's love language is physical affection. Receive affection when it is offered. Melt into the moment. There will be some temptation to move out of the moment, believing everything else is more important. This will starve your relationship. Take a moment to stroke, hug, wink, nuzzle, compliment, or touch.

Boost Your Sex IQ: 17 Tips to Transform Sex From Mundane to Mind Blowing

These humor-infused tips improve you as a lover. If your love-making has become robotic, it's time to refresh it with sexual IQ.

1. Introduce spatial and sensory novelty. There's nothing like monotony to kill the sex buzz. Avoid having sex at the same time and in the same place. Initiating standard sex fare at 10:30 pm after an exhausting day in the same room every time threatens even the most committed couple's libido. The laundry room offers sturdy appliances. Try it out in the kitchen or bathroom. Clear off that kitchen table pronto. If you can't stand the thought of getting busy in family spaces, prime your bedroom for sexy-time. Buy new sheets. Use peppermint or rose oil in a homemade room spray or diffuse

something sensual like jasmine. Buy a fabulous rug. Light candles. Make sure there's a mirror or two nearby for some visual wow. Stick some mirrored tiles on your ceiling. Yoga mats do wonders for traction. They are not just for the downward dog. A Liberator® sex wedge gets you in all the right angles. Missionary is so vanilla. Take your sex from mundane to mischief. Did I mention the great outdoors is a stimulating place for novel sex?

2. <u>Do you still flirt with your partner?</u> You are not roommates, so shake those tail feathers. Flirt with your partner using the triangle gaze (let your eyes glide from eye to eye to mouth to eyes). Eye contact is always important for intimacy but can be especially erotic during sex. You can use your eyes to create a shocking amount of sexual tension. Pair this with deep rhythmic breathing (research tantric breathing) and you've got a winner. Lick your lips while your partner is looking and drive them wild. Use sexual tension as a warm-up. Use the triangle gaze to convey where your mind is at to your partner. Or, let your eyes fuse with theirs for a moment and gently drag your gaze down their body, then back to their eyes. Practice makes perfect. To pull this off, you must work on confidence and self-love. Practice feeling good about who you are and what you have to offer.

3. <u>Phys Ed</u>. Use the technique of hovering. Hovering means being physically close to your partner in a suggestive manner, but not touching. Do the same with a kiss, practicing keeping just out of their reach. Remember that sexual tension is built with the smallest of gestures. Softly run your finger down your partner's spine. Gently place your hand in the small of your partner's back. Tuck their hair behind their

ears. Cup their chin in your hands. Small gestures are strong turn-ons. The neck and ears are highly charged and accessible. Use skin to your advantage.

4. <u>Words of affirmation</u>. Give your partner three compliments per day. Stop the distractions and be mindful of how great they really are.

5. <u>Play therapy</u>. Approach your bedroom like a lion cub. Schedule time for play in the bedroom, not just sex! There should be time for cuddling, lazing, reading, talking, nibbling, laughing, tickling, play fighting, and resting together. Schedule day-bed dates. Have you watched how lion cubs play? Emulate this in your bedroom. Turn off the TV and your devices and turn to your partner instead. Remember the good old days where you spent hours (maybe even days) together in bed?

6. <u>The sexy side of cellular</u>. Send a sexy or suggestive text now and again, maybe with a promise to meet your partner at the door naked. Avoid sending texts to discuss serious concerns. Save that for a face-to-face conversation. Facetime® with full or partial nudity. Check the number. You don't want *those* credentials going to the wrong inbox.

7. <u>Booty budget</u>. Make room in your budget for erotica that enhances your intimacy. Explore. The only limits in your sex life are the ones you set. Enhance your sensual side with lingerie, candles, and massage oils. Splurge on luxury sheets. Buy technique books, sex game boards, or dice games. Find novels that arouse your interest in sex. Indulge in couples porn. Buy good quality sex toys. You'll be amazed at what's

out there. The Picobong® is a gender-neutral sex toy that you will find on Amazon.com. Everybody wins with this new gadget. Oh, and make sure you have lots of really good lube. Good lube prevents chafing and UTI's. Vibrant Health Company endorses UberLube®. Just the right kind of slippery and staying power without the goo. Don't limit the lube to your genitals. Slather all over for a super slippery, sexy and shiny bod.

8. <u>To do list.</u> Make a sex bucket list. Share it with your partner. Work your way down the list.

9. <u>Screen-play</u>. Record a sexy movie of you and your partner. Watch back without being critical of your body.

10. <u>Love locks</u>. Hair is incredibly sexually charged. Play with or gently pull your partner's hair. I'm not just talking about the hair on your head. Use your hair to enhance your sex experience.

11. <u>Laws of attraction</u>. Explore the laws of attraction in your relationship. Take turns with your partner. Describe what attracts you to them. Have them tell you why they are attracted to you. Then make one to three requests each that would increase attraction. Write them down. Follow through.

12. <u>Parallel play without a traffic light</u>. Indulge in mutual masturbation without penetration (this means to bringing each other to climax). Another idea is to bring yourself to climax as your partner observes. Avoid what I call the traffic light method of sex. The traffic light method of sex is the kiss-grab-penetrate method. It is the predictable and stale 1-2-3 sequence of kiss to foreplay to penetration. It's akin to a

turkey sandwich: great for the first few days of your lunch, but boring after that. Another idea to avoid the traffic light method is to put orgasm off limits as a strategy to increase desire. Engage in sexual play but stop just short of orgasm or ejaculation. Stay right on the edge for a while, return to caressing, and head back toward orgasm. See if you can use this method several times before you let yourself dive into a powerful finish. Set a date on your calendar for intercourse and look forward to the finale as you egg each other on in the hours or days leading up to your playtime. Let the sexual tension build.

13. <u>Mystery spot</u>. Find your partner's erogenous zones: ears, nape of the neck, small of the back, armpits, back of the wrists, inner thigh. Kiss, lick, and nibble your way through the menu.

14. **<u>Music is the food of love</u>**. Make a sexy-time playlist. Music can be a great backdrop for love-making.

15. <u>Valedictorian</u>. Education on all things sex is important. Knowledge is power. Know your toys, know your positions, and know your techniques. Don't know your dildo from your rabbit? Thought a butt plug was something to prevent the runs? Think a spreader bar is something for butter? Did you know the clitoris now has its own suction toy? Do your research at some of the sites listed later in this book. An awesome new performer on the sex toys market is what I refer to as the clit whisperer. It's called "SONA Cruise". You can purchase it at lelo.com. Equip yourself with the buzzwords so that you know how to talk with your partner. Be your own sexpert and know the lingo. Review the Urban Dictionary occasionally for updates. There are lots of ways to tell your partner you want them. Sex is also described as

laying pipe, shooting the sherbet, dining in the Y, humping, bottoming, and topping. Rimming and pegging are fairly new terms even though the technique is as old as humankind. There are truly only six basic sex positions, but just like Twister, the variations are endless.

16. <u>Arriving early</u>. When they come too soon, and you could go on for hours, you might need to learn how to delay ejaculation. Premature ejaculation can be downright disheartening. It's common, and there are techniques to solve this problem. Topical anesthetics can be applied to the head of the penis to minimize stimulation and delay ejaculation. For some, a cock ring helps. Many couples find the squeeze technique helpful. The squeeze technique takes dedication and patience on both you and your partner's part. Practice the technique every week or so over the next few months. Have sex without practicing it, also. Relax and breathe through anxiety. Be kind to each other. The basic idea is for your partner to position their fingers in the right way on the penis. Instructions and videos can be found online. The point here is communication. The penis must be squeezed immediately before ejaculation occurs and since your partner cannot guess, they must be informed. The idea is to squeeze before they come, several times in a row if possible, before finally allowing a free-flowing ejaculation. Read "The Ejaculation Trainer" (Gorden, M. (2014) Brandon Hardwick Master) available on Amazon.com for a review of techniques that go beyond the simple squeeze. Since females need direct clitoral stimulation to orgasm, coming too soon can be avoided by simply easing up on the clitoris. Premature ejaculation or 'coming too soon' is mostly a penis related issue.

17. <u>Talk dirty to me</u>. Absolutely nothing drives you crazy more than a partner that knows how to talk to you when you're

shagging (forgive the slang, but I'm British. I had to slip this in somewhere). If intimacy is comprised of sex and communication, imagine what happens when you pair the two together. You might feel shy about speaking to your partner during sex, even if you are an extrovert in every other situation. Please practice being able to communicate while you're doing the deed. If you want to send them straight to heaven, practice talking dirty. No one else will ever know.

Vibrant Health Company's Favorite Books on Sex

She Comes First- Kerner, I. (2009) New York, NY: Harper Collins.   (Author's note- All cis-males should read this!)

Becoming Cliterate- Mintz, L. (2017) New York, NY: Harper One.

Hot Monogamy- Love, P. & Robinson, J. (1995) New York, NY: Penguin.

Hot Sex: Over 200 Things You Can Try Tonight- Morse, E. & Waxman, J. (2011) San Francisco, CA: Weldon-Owen.

Assisted Loving- Morris, B. (2008) New York, NY: Harper Collins.

Vibrant Health Company's Favorite Web Sites on Sex

https://www.babeland.com/

https://www.goodinbed.com/

https://www.lelo.com/

https://www.adameve.com/

https://www.omgyes.com/

Chapter 6

The Body Positive Movement

"Ultimately, we delay our sense of self and ease in the world if we refuse to accept the magic of our body, TODAY. There was a time when you didn't judge your body. Recapture that. Enjoy what you have." ~ Traci Baxendale Ball

Body Love: Reclaiming Your Sexual and Sensual Self

Low libido and body hate are issues across all genders. Cis-females, in particular, report distress in balancing life roles with the sexual needs of their partner. Here are suggestions for you if you want to feel more integrated and at peace with your body.

Food and Body Gratitude

Food and sensuality are a fine pairing. Food can be a great source of pleasure. Think of how many rituals involve food all over the world. But food may be a source of great anxiety. Food is a source of concern and even pain for many of you. This is reflected in your body image. Food can be restricted in an effort to starve your body. Similarly, you may be prone to overfeeding your body when you experience stress. Our culture's emphasis on "thin equals healthy" and "diet equals thin" has culminated in a loss of pleasure and pride in your body as well as conflict with food.

Feeling sexual means feeling good about the body you have. Feeling good about the body you have means you see food as restorative and enjoyable. Understand that to transform your sex life you must increase your desire for sex or your libido. To increase libido, you must have a body positive attitude. To have a body positive attitude, you must do good for your body; which means doing the best you can.

When food is balanced in your life, it's easier to cultivate body gratitude.

Here is some radical advice: do not diet. Restriction turns into a lifestyle which increases the misery around eating. Deprivation induces binging. Learn mindful eating from "Why Diets Make

Us Fat". (Aamodt, S. (2016) New York, NY: Penguin) Read the book or watch the TED talk by Sandra Aamodt. Find a mindful eating coach or a counselor. You can also attend a support group. Over time your body will reach its set point range, and you won't feel the constant urge to restrict or binge. You will eat when you need to, and you will eat what you want. You can eat clean *enough,* yet eat in a way that elicits a powerful dopamine response (pleasure, satiation) from your favorite food. Most importantly, your inner dialog has to shift from, "I hate (this part of my body)", to focusing on what you are grateful for. Shifting the self-talk is learned through the practice of cognitive therapy. It's all about noticing when you beat yourself up and deciding to play nice in your own sandbox.

In summary, I am asking you to make friends with food.

While we are on the subject of food, cooking with your partner can be a very intimate, fun activity. Don't miss an opportunity to turn these daily musts into daily lusts. This applies to your shower and cleaning routine also. Invite your partner in to wash your back. If you've not done housework naked, it's time to give it a whirl.

Recommendations for Body Love - Support for BodyPositive

In addition to feeling more connected to vitality through mindful use of food, here are some other suggestions for body love:

- **Love the Skin You're In**
  Take some time to make a list of activities you can do every week that will increase your connection to your body, heighten awareness of your femininity or masculinity (where applicable), and awaken your sexual being. Start with a goal to hit three activities per week

and slowly increase to one daily.

o   Small load tasks: A sensual shower, or commitments such as, "I will take the time to comb my hair before bed.", or "I will use a nice smelling lotion to hydrate and appreciate my skin.", or "I will look in the mirror every day and notice something I do like."

o   Medium load tasks: "I will stretch for 10 minutes every other day and connect to my body and breath." Dance to a great song, sing out loud, or find an app for a five-minute meditation. Find a way to be just a bit silly every day.

o   Bigger load tasks: "I will give myself a mani/pedi/facial at home.", "I will make a salt or sugar facial scrub or homemade soap, and use them in the shower.", or "I will read a racy romance novel."

- **Jump-Start Your Sex Drive**
  You can jump-start your sex drive and desire with erotic tools such as books, magazines, and movies that are designed to appeal to couples. The market for couples has come (no pun intended) a long way from bad porn. Many tasteful online merchants cater to the couples market (lelo.com, goodvibes.com, adameve.com, and evesgarden.com are good examples).

- **Clit ed, Penis Savvy**
  I've included diagrams for you. They will help you navigate your sex ed. Masturbation is good for you. Self-exploration is encouraged.
  Let's talk about the Big O. Guys first. Things are pretty easy to find on the penis. It's all you need for

orgasm and it's a straight shot to stimulate it, though I'd encourage you to explore other options. Despite the fact that it's a straight shot, different folks like different strokes. You need to ask your partner how they like their penis stimulated. Ask your partner what kind of penile stroke they like during your sexy time. Sometimes they will be in the mood for a soft, rhythmic stroke. Sometimes a tighter grip with quicker hand (or mouth) action will be preferred.

The outer genitalia of the female is a little more complex. The clitoris is the only path to orgasm for most women. It is also the only piece of anatomy known to science to exist exclusively for the sake of pleasure. Generally speaking, the clitoris enjoys a soft touch and moist conditions to begin activity. One of the most common complaints about sex toys is that the stimulation they produce is too firm for the clitoris.

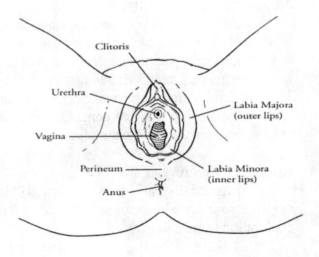

Some days you're too busy to pee, so I am sure that learning the anatomy of your body takes a backseat when it comes to your to-do list. It is a fact that many people have never actually studied their genitals in a mirror. Females often don't know where their urethra is located in comparison to the clitoris and vaginal opening. Locate your parts on the diagrams provided.

If you've forgotten you even have a piece of your anatomy that is a source of sexual pleasure, take time to explore and cultivate it. Remember that cis-females need direct clitoral stimulation to orgasm. This means it's not likely she will orgasm during penetrative intercourse, especially when the good vibes of NRE are long gone. Practice masturbation alone as well as with your partner and experiment with what makes you squeal with delight. Maybe it's more like a roar for you. If you would like instructions, check out the sex ed on the very polished website: https://www.omgyes.com. Have you thought of using a small clitoral stimulator that you can wear discreetly during the day that'll get you feeling steamy before you even punch out of work? Some experts claim the clitoris will be de-sensitized with the use of a vibrator or other devices. I encourage you to mix it up and sometimes masturbate the organic way - without batteries. If you have a penis, experimenting with masturbation is just as important for you. More so if there are issues with premature ejaculation, ED, or low libido. Use generous helpings of lube and some visual stimulation. Do your thing.

- **Vag Gym: Beyond Kegels**
Getting your pelvic floor in good shape is empowering. You will feel more integrated with your body. This will

help you experience the self as a sensual and sexual being. Plus - no more sneeze squirts. Bonus! Kegels are good for all genders. Females find strengthening their pelvic floor improves sensations during intercourse. This is good for the penis in your life (where applicable). They say a mind stretched by experience can never go back to its old dimensions. Don't apply this metaphor to your anatomy after childbirth or other life experiences that weaken the pelvic floor. Work to get those internal parts back into shape. Pelvic floor strength and core work is important for your overall health. Clients ask whether or not they should use a Kegel exerciser. And what about Ben-Wa balls or Venus balls? Many devices and appliances exist to strengthen the pelvic floor and vaginal walls. Some experts claim these products can have adverse effects and damage your vaginal strength. Who is right? Opinions vary, so do your research. Pelvic floor PT is a medical specialty. Check with your physician about a referral. If you don't want to use a device, you can work with a personal trainer. There are various yoga poses, Pilates® moves, and core strength exercises that help. If you notice a burn after sex, some products help cool the vulva area and reduce inflammation or irritation. I recommend VagiKool® for an ultra-soothing vag chill.

- **You're Too Sexy for Your Shirt**
  You are a visual creature. You appreciate it if you're partner looks and smells good. Keep up on your appearance. Brush your teeth. Sex appeal and clothes go hand in hand. Remember we talked about acting-into how you want to feel? If you want to feel confident, adopt a look you can rock. If you want to feel sexy, think about how to achieve this with what you wear. Is your entire wardrobe the definition of slinky or is it shades of grey?

Have you bought new sexy underwear recently? If you had to hang your laundry out to dry, would you be stuffing those off-white undies in your pockets as your hot neighbor walks past? You'll soon remember that you own rights to a very pleasurable part of your body if you dress it up a bit.

- **Creativity and Sensuality Are Closely Linked**
  Read, journal, draw, create anything. Explore planetsark.com for inspiration on being a succulent wild woman. A client once told me the art is 80's, but the ideas are timeless. Laughter, fun, and taking small risks can be gateways to increased libido. Follow Julia Cameron on Facebook to dip your toe into your own creative waters. Free up some of that stuck and frozen mental space and shake up that sex drive. The idea is to feel beautiful as you connect to your higher self.

- **Fantasy Life**
  Engage readily in sexual fantasy. Need ideas on where to start with some titillating audio/visual material? Have a peek here: https://www.lelo.com/blog/erotic-fantasies/.

- **Learn Mindfulness**
  You've heard a lot about mindfulness, meditation, and visualization. These practices can be called upon to awaken your sensual self. There are free apps and free YouTube clips and courses. My favorite resource is a website called Trans4Mind. Being mindful will help you be more aware of your body AND your partner's. Meditating will help keep that inner lake calm.

- **Beef Up on Sex Skills**
  Do you feel you lack some knowledge in the sex ed

department? No worries. You can learn. Explore the website goodinbed.com for practical tips on a better sex life so you can step into those sheets with confidence. Check out Babeland's articles at https://www.babeland.com/sexinfo/features to be a sex genius.

- **Anxious About Your Penis Size?**
  The length or girth of your penis is not correlated with being a good lover. Know that it's what you do with that pecker that counts. If there's room in there once you're 'all in', focus on movement (circles, thrusting) for stimulation where it counts. Adjust your position and experiment with what feels good for both of you. You have two hands. Use them to add stimulation to where your partner likes it. The whole body is a wonderland.

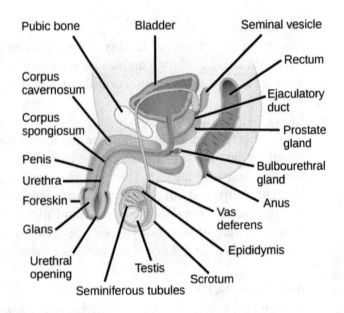

- **Do What You Do Best**
  Think of the times you feel most sexy and alive. Is it
  when you swim? Is it listening to certain music? When
  you dance? When you laugh? When you're out in nature?
  When you wear certain clothes? How can you recreate
  that feeling more in the life you have today? Do what you
  love more. Notice your joy. Pull your partner into that
  moment with you. Go get 'em tiger!

**Why Your Technique and Your Body are Only Part of Your
Love Story**

We've reviewed how important it is to get comfortable with
your body. If you do your work in this area, you'll approach all
interactions with your mate from a centered, confident stance.
We've also talked about technique. I've suggested how you can
improve your sexual IQ. In long-term relationships, people forget
how to flirt actively. There is a decrease over time in your sexual
identity as other roles or hats you wear in life zap energy.
Remembering some simple techniques to increase sexual tension
is key to reclaiming your relationship's sexual heat. The
behaviors that supported that New Relationship Energy, or early
romantic love, do get left by the wayside; lost in between the
responsibilities of jobs and family. Infidelity is often attributed to
'lackluster' intimacy, an absence of novelty, and infrequency of
sex.

Sex must be sustained. Whatever the obstacle, find a way to
work through it.

A cautionary tale. Technique alone cannot improve the level
of satisfaction in your sex life. It's one thing to choreograph your
sexual dynamics. It's another thing entirely to put your heart and
soul into it. Study after study has shown that what maintains our
interest in sex in long-term monogamous relationships is how

our partner responds. The most visually pleasing partner with the best technique would be unappealing if they had no physical or emotional response during lovemaking. Think about how you can improve your response to your partner *as well as* learning techniques. Think about how you show your partner you want them *as well as* resurrecting those moves that seemed to naturally occur as a result of the early physical attraction.

We Create Love and Intimacy in Our Long-Term Relationships.

Notice the word *create*. It implies an active process. We have to actively mold sexual heat by our actions, and we must recognize it's our responsibility to do so.

Take responsibility for the love in your relationship! Now get out there and make your partner your 'new' lover!

"There are two primary choices in life: to accept conditions as they exist, or accept the responsibility for changing them."
~ Denis Waitley

Author Bio

Professional Experience

Traci is a nationally recognized mental health expert, speaker, writer, and entrepreneur. She began her career in England in 1992 and holds degrees from universities in the UK and the USA. She is the founder of Vibrant Health Company LLC and its related brands. She maintains a full-time private practice, which includes an innovative virtual clinic that has been part of several national research studies on emerging practices. She has specialties in trauma, addictions, and sex ed. Stigma-free and GSD competent, her unique brands and groundbreaking written materials encourage all persons to reach their potential. Traci advocates for self-help, professional counseling, and the pursuit of the best wellness possible in spite of age, injury, and illness. She writes freelance on topics of mental health, wellness, and relationships. You can find her work on her website at https://vibranthealthcompany.com/, on the authoritative mindfulness hub at Trans4Mind https://trans4mind.com/ and Better Help https://www.betterhelp.com/advice/. Heavily influenced by a holistic perspective, Traci consistently researches nutrition and alternative approaches to health. This research informs her practice and somatic bodywork. A Master's prepared clinician, she also holds advanced credentials in various specialties. She maintains certifications/licenses in six fitness formats and instructs students in her hometown, living out the conviction that mind-body approaches offer the most effective pathway to mental health.

Education

Traci has a BA(Hons) in Psychology from the University of Sheffield, England. She has an MSW from Western Michigan University. She holds a CAADC (Certified Advanced Alcohol and Drug Counselor) credential. She was inducted as a member of the American Academy for Experts in Traumatic Stress in the early 2000's.

Philosophy on Mental Health and Wellness

Mental health and wellness is a lifelong journey that is punctuated by struggle, illness, injury, obstacles, and often times trauma. No human being escapes the reality of suffering. It's something to which we can all relate. It's something we can survive too! I believe in the resilience of human nature, the power of connection with others, the importance of loving who you are, and the value of vulnerability. It's crucial that we don't underestimate how simple pleasures such as a good laugh, a good meal, or a beautiful sunrise can boost our ability to cope. I understand that some persons will have chronic mental health issues that are incapacitating for years, while others will experience anxiety and depression only temporarily. Whatever the case, I meet my clients and readers where they are with compassion and understanding, as well as the belief that I am here to learn from them. My overarching philosophy is "We are in this together. Let's see what we can get done."

Traci Baxendale Ball LMSW, CAADC
Founder-Vibrant Health Company LLC

CPSIA information can be obtained
at www.ICGtesting.com
Printed in the USA
FSHW021431090419

9 780692 065518